'The cheese is brought
to the table with the mites
or maggots round it so thick
that they bring a spoon with
them to eat the mites with,
as you do the cheese'

Daniel Defoe, describing his visit to Stilton

GEORGIAN COOKERY

Recipes & History

by
Jennifer Stead

with a Foreword by
Loyd Grossman OBE

ENGLISH HERITAGE

Front cover: High Life, 1764, by Thomas Rowlandson

Endpapers: An elegant dinner of seven and nine dishes, using the recipes in this book

Published by English Heritage, Kemble Drive, Swindon SN2 2GZ

Copyright © English Heritage and Jennifer Stead
First published 1985
Revised edition 2003

ISBN 1 85074 869 1

C60, 1/04, Product code 50816

Edited by Susan Kelleher
Designed by Pauline Hull
Picture research by Elaine Willis
Brought to press by Andrew McLaren and Elaine Pooke
Printed in England by Bath Press

CONTENTS

FOREWORD

Would the pyramids have been built without the recently invented bread to efficiently feed the workforce? Food is a common denominator between us all, and a potent link with our ancestors, just as much as an ancient parish church or a listed house.

I am delighted to contribute a Foreword to English Heritage's series of historic cookery books, which neatly combine two of my passions – history and food. Most of us no longer have to catch or grow our own food before eating it, but the continuing daily need for sustenance still powerfully links us with our earliest forebears. We may not like the thought of Roman fish sauce made with fermented entrails (until we next add oyster sauce to a Chinese beef dish), but we can only sigh with recognition at a Jacobean wife's exhortation to 'let yor butter bee scalding hott in yor pan' before pouring in the beaten eggs for an omelette. The Roman penchant for dormice cooked in milk doesn't resonate with us now, but a dish of pears in red wine features at modern dinner parties just as it did in medieval times.

Food and cooking have inevitably changed down the centuries, as modern cookers have supplanted open hearths, and increased wealth and speedy transport have opened up modern tastes and palates to the widest range of ingredients and cuisines. But it's worth remembering that it was the Romans who gave us onions, sugar was an expensive luxury in the 16th century as was tea in the 17th, the tomato only became popular in Europe in the 19th century and even in the 1950s avocados and red peppers were still exotic foreign imports.

I urge you to experiment with the recipes in these books which cover over 2,000 years, and hope you enjoy, as I have, all that is sometimes strange and often familiar about the taste of times past.

Loyd Grossman OBE
Former Commissioner of English Heritage
Chairman of the Campaign for Museums

INTRODUCTION

In 1700 the English still lived and ate in a way that would have seemed familiar to their medieval ancestors: agricultural, self-sufficient, killing cattle in winter, eating thick pottages. By 1800 England was on the brink of the modern era, seeing a widespread move off the land into the towns, the rise of a prosperous middle class, the development of newspapers and advertising, and the birth of a consumer society.

In 1700 most kitchen equipment was simple, made locally by blacksmith, whitesmith or potter. By 1800 there was on the market a huge variety of kitchen equipment, tools, pots, dishes and glasses. At the beginning of the century a housewife might buy one pan. By the end, she might purchase a whole set. Technological discoveries in one field were often applied to others. For example, improvements in rolling sheet iron, which produced better kitchen utensils, also produced finer flour when the rolling process was seized upon by millers. And new eating and drinking habits were a spur to new design in the metal and pottery industries – habits such as the eating of soup, or the drinking of tea and coffee.

Recipes

DISHES MADE BY ALL CLASSES

PLAIN PUDDING

Puddings boiled or baked, sweet, plain or savoury, formed a major part of 18th-century fare. Plain pudding is simply pancake batter boiled in a cloth (plain and suet puddings are actually lighter when boiled in a cloth, because they can expand in all directions). The same batter baked in a tin under roasting meat becomes Yorkshire pudding. On 13 February 1757 Thomas Turner dined on hog's cheek and vegetables with a 'plain batter pudding', all boiled. Parson Woodforde regaled his parishioners on Tithe Audit-day 1799 with boiled and roast meat and plenty of plum and plain puddings. Mrs Raffald's pudding is simple to make, and very good.

50 g (2 oz) plain flour
1.5 ml (¹/₄ tsp) salt
3 eggs
225 ml (8 fl oz) milk or single cream

For this size of pudding make a 45 cm (18 in) square pudding cloth of white cotton or doubled muslin. Boil a large pan of water and put an old plate in the bottom. Drop the pudding cloth in briefly, lift it out with a wooden spoon and let it drape over the spoon handle placed across a pan to drip. Have ready a piece of string. Sift the flour and salt into a bowl. In another bowl beat the eggs well. Add the flour, salt and milk and beat to make a thin batter. Squeeze out

9

the pudding cloth, lay it on the table and sprinkle well with flour, gently shaking off the excess. To support the cloth while filling it, lay it in a basin with the floured side up, pour in the batter, gather up the corners and all the edges (leaving room for the pudding to expand), tie securely with string and place in a pan of boiling water, which must cover the pudding at all times. Cover the pan, leaving a small gap, and boil for 30 minutes. Lift the pudding out and dip briefly in cold water to loosen the cloth. Place in a colander, untie the string and peel back the cloth. Place a heated dish over the pudding, reverse the colander and gently peel away the rest of the cloth. Serve at once with meat, or as a dessert with hot wine sauce (see p 37).

Elizabeth Raffald:
The experienced English housekeeper

BUTTERED WHEAT OR BARLEY

Dishes of this convenient food were still being sold in the streets of London in the mid-18th century. The hulled wheat or barley was pre-boiled to a jelly, then reheated on the spot with butter, sugar and spice, usually nutmeg. The buttering of cereals had been common since Tudor times.

50 g (2 oz) pearl barley
1.1 l (2 pt) water
50 g (2 oz) butter
15 ml (1 tbls) sugar
a pinch of nutmeg

Simmer the barley and water together in a saucepan until the barley is very tender. Drain. Reheat the drained barley with the butter, sugar and nutmeg, then serve.

Hannah Glasse:
The art of cookery made plain and easy

BARLEY GRUEL

Barley gruel, or 'plumb porridge', was a common dish and tastes very good. It is similar to frumenty but less rich. (Frumenty or furmity was usually made with hulled wheat, enriched with milk, cream and egg yolks, and in many areas remained up until the 20th century a special Christmas dish.)

1.1 l (2 pt) water
50 g (2 oz) pearl barley
25 g (1 oz) raisins
25 g (1 oz) currants
2.5 ml (½ tsp) ground mace
30 ml (2 tbls) sugar
50 ml (2 fl oz) white wine

Put the water in a saucepan with the barley, raisins, currants and mace, and boil until the water is reduced by half and the barley is tender. Stir in the sugar and white wine, and serve.

Hannah Glasse:
The art of cookery made plain and easy

This dish can be made in advance and reheated when required.

WATER GRUEL

To make water gruel: 'Take a Pint of Water, and a large Spoonful of Oatmeal, stir it together, let it boil up three or four times, stirring it often. Don't let it boil over, then strain it through a sieve, salt it to your Palate, put in a good Piece of fresh Butter, brue [stir] it with a Spoon till the Butter is all melted, and it will be fine and smooth, and very good. Some love a little Pepper in it.'

This light but sustaining dish was eaten by all classes. The well-off ate it with wine sauce and buttered toast, added plumped currants and raisins, sugar, mace and sack (sherry), or took it plain for breakfast or as an invalid food.

Although water gruel was eaten hot, when allowed to go cold it sets into an oatmeal flummery, which is equally good eaten with sugar and light cream.

450 ml (16 fl oz) water
20 ml (1 heaped tbls) oatmeal
15 g (½ oz) butter
a pinch of salt

Put the water and the oatmeal in a saucepan and bring to the boil, stirring. Boil for 2 minutes, stirring occasionally. Strain through a sieve into an individual bowl or mug, add butter and salt, and eat with a spoon.

Hannah Glasse:
The art of cookery made plain and easy

WHEY

Curds and whey was still eaten in the early 18th century. It was junket, made from milk rennet and eaten in a dish with sugar, cream and flavourings such as nutmeg and rosewater. But during the century this dish gradually lost favour as unrenneted fresh cream confections became more and more fashionable. Curds and whey (junket) is easily made today using rennet essence, following the instructions given on the bottle.

Whey as a drink (sometimes called whig) was popular in many dairying districts, and it was also sold in the streets of large towns. Many people made whey at home by curdling blue (skimmed) milk with cream of tartar or other acids, such as old verjuice (a condiment made from sour apples) or juice of scurvy grass.

150 ml (¹/₄ pt) skimmed milk
15 ml (1 tbls) fresh lemon juice or
**   30 ml (2 tbls) fresh orange juice**

Reconstituted dried milk can be used for this recipe. Heat the milk until tepid (21°C/70°F), then add the lemon or orange juice. Leave in a warm place for at least 10 minutes to curdle. Strain through a fine sieve or muslin, or *'pour the whey clear off, and sweeten to your Palate.'*

Hannah Glasse:
The art of cookery made plain and easy

Whey makes a refreshing drink, especially when chilled. You can eat the curds, mixed with sugar, cream and nutmeg, with fresh soft fruit.

PLUM POTTAGE

The old traditional rich plum pottage, which had been made especially for feasts and festivals, came to be associated in the later 17th century principally with Christmas. It continued to be made well into the 18th century (and as late as the 19th in Scotland). Hannah Glasse calls it 'plum-porridge' which indicates its thick consistency. By now, the actual meat was not used in the dish, only the broth, and the mixture was beginning to resemble a rather sloppy plum pudding. The modern very rich Christmas pudding developed from this liquor-laced porridge only in the 19th century. The 'plum puddings' eaten on Christmas Day in the 18th century (for example by Thomas Turner and Parson Woodforde) were just ordinary plum puddings. Hannah Glasse comments that the beef broth may be thickened with sago instead of breadcrumbs. Lady Grisell Baillie used the newly fashionable sago in Scotland on Christmas Day 1715 to thicken her Christmas plum pottage, which was served as part of the first course. (You can do this using 75 g (3 oz) sago to 850 ml (1½ pt) broth and simmering for 15 minutes.)

1–1.4 kg (2–3 lb) shin of beef
1.1–1.4 l (2–2½ pt) water
125 g (4 oz) fresh white breadcrumbs
200 g (7 oz) mixed dried fruit (currants, raisins, dates, cooked prunes)
5 ml (1 tsp) grated nutmeg
1.5 ml (¼ tsp) ground mace
1.5 ml (¼ tsp) ground cloves

2.5 ml (¹/₂ tsp) cinnamon
a pinch of salt
75 ml (3 fl oz) sherry
75 ml (3 fl oz) port
juice of 1 Seville orange or
  lemon, to serve

Simmer the beef in the water, covered, for about 2 hours until tender. Strain it and keep the meat for another dish. Add the breadcrumbs to 850 ml (1¹/₂ pt) of the broth and soak for 1 hour. Then stir in the fruit, spices and salt and bring to the boil. Add the sherry and port and simmer, uncovered, until the fruit is plump (about 15 minutes). Serve hot in individual bowls, with the juice of the Seville orange or lemon.

John Nott:
The cook's and confectioner's dictionary

DISHES MADE BY THE
TRADESMAN CLASS AND ABOVE

GREEN PEA SOUP

Pease pottage, or pease pudding, made with field peas, was once a national dish. At the turn of the 18th century the gentry and middle classes began to scorn thick pottages as labourers' food, preferring the new elegant French dish called soup. Soup was a 'remove' dish – always set at the head of the table and eaten first, then removed to make way for fish. This typical recipe was a way of using over-mature garden peas. If you have none, use split peas.

575 ml (1 pt) old garden peas or 225 g (8 oz) split peas
850 ml (1½ pt) water
a little celery, chopped
a little onion, chopped
a pinch of ground mace
a pinch of ground cloves
a pinch of black pepper
1.4 l (2½ pt) good meat or vegetable stock
350 g (12 oz) fresh or frozen young peas
6 slices French bread and clarified butter (see p 37), to serve

If using split peas, soak them in 850 ml (1½ pt) water overnight. Then simmer the split peas or old garden peas in the water with the celery and onion, mace, cloves and black pepper, covered, until tender. Mash, sieve or blend, then add this pulp to the stock. Just before serving, heat the soup, add the fresh young peas, and simmer until tender. If using frozen peas, simmer no longer than 3 minutes. Serve with slices of French bread fried in clarified butter floating in each bowl, or, as Mrs Glasse puts it: *Let a fried French roll swim in it.*

Hannah Glasse:
The art of cookery made plain and easy

If time is short, a 430 g (15 oz) can of pease pudding may be used instead of the cooked old or split peas.

'Of soup and love, the first is the best'

Thomas Fuller
Gnomologia, 1732

POTTED VENISON

Potted meats and fish were popular during the 17th and 18th centuries as side dishes for a second course. Potting is a good way to preserve these foods for several weeks. Game, particularly venison, was highly prized because, through enclosures and harsh game laws, it had become scarce. Game could be bought in London markets, but much of it was probably poached. The venison in shops today has not usually been hung till 'gamey'. Many large country houses had outdoor game larders, where game could be hung for several weeks before being eaten.

800–900 g (1³/₄–2 lb) piece of rolled venison shoulder with fat
75 g (3 oz) butter

45 ml (3 tbls) flour
2.5 ml (¹/₂ tsp) salt
2.5 ml (¹/₂ tsp) black pepper
5 ml (1 tsp) ground mace
2.5 ml (¹/₂ tsp) ground cloves
10 ml (2 tsps) grated nutmeg
6 anchovy fillets

Put the meat in an ovenproof lidded pot that is only just big enough to hold it. Cut the butter in pieces and lay on the meat. To seal the lid, make a huff paste by mixing the flour with enough water to make a dough that can be moulded round the lid edge. Bake at gas mark 1, 140°C, 275°F for 3–4 hours, or until a sharp fork goes in easily. Leave until cool. Lift the meat clear of the juices into a large bowl, and tear the meat to fine shreds with the fingers, discarding any gristle, bone and fat. Then mash the meat finely in a pestle and mortar (or use a blender) until light and dry. Add seasoning and spices. Mash the anchovies finely in 75–90 ml (5–6 tbls) melted fat from the cooking pot, or use freshly melted clarified butter (see p 37), and incorporate with the meat. (Do not include any meat juices as the meat would not then keep.) Press the meat well down in a clean dry pot, to exclude all the air. Pour more melted fat on top to seal completely. Serve in slices, with pickles.

Gluttony, by Thomas Rowlandson

Hannah Glasse:
The art of cookery made plain and easy

STEWED VENISON

To stew venison in claret: 'Cut your Venison into slices, put it into a stew-pan, with a little claret, a Sprig or two of Rosemary, half a dozen cloves, a little Vinegar, Sugar and grated Bread; when these have stw'd some time, grate in some Nutmeg, and serve it up.'

John Nott would have cooked his stew in a stew-pan or 'casserole' (a French utensil) on a brick-built stewing stove. Those without stoves would use a chafing-dish of charcoal on the hearth, or would cook their stew in a covered jar inside a cauldron of boiling water.

900 g (2 lb) stewing venison or beef
6 whole cloves
5 ml (1 tsp) rosemary
5 ml (1 tsp) salt
5 ml (1 tsp) black pepper
20 ml (4 tsps) wine vinegar
450 ml (16 fl oz) red wine
10 ml (2 tsps) sugar
275 ml (¹/₂ pt) good stock
50 g (2 oz) fresh white breadcrumbs
a little grated nutmeg
orange slices to garnish

Cut the meat into 4 cm (1¹/₂ in) pieces. Then stew all the ingredients, except the nutmeg, together, covered, very gently for 2 hours. About 15 minutes before serving, stir in a grating of nutmeg. Garnish with sliced oranges.

John Nott:
The cook's and confectioner's dictionary

FINE SAUSAGES

450 g (1 lb) pork mince
100 g (4 oz) suet
15–30 ml (1–2 tbls) finely chopped fresh sage
grated rind of 1 lemon
7.5 ml ('/2 tbls) chopped fresh parsley
7.5 ml ('/2 tbls) chopped fresh marjoram
half a nutmeg, grated
5 ml (1 tsp) ground black pepper
2.5 ml ('/2 tsp) salt
1 egg, beaten

Place mince and all other ingredients, except the egg, in a large bowl. Mix together very well (this is easiest done with your hands) then add the egg and mix this in. Shape the mixture into small sausage shapes with your hands. Heat 15–30 ml (1–2 tbls) oil in a large frying pan, then cook the sausages over a medium heat, turning regularly, until browned all over and cooked through.

Hannah Glasse:
The art of cookery made plain and easy

JUGGED PIGEONS

Pigeons were plentiful, many large houses having their own dovecotes, and were valuable fresh meat in winter. The process of jugging goes back to medieval times when several pots and puddings would be economically cooked together in a large cauldron of boiling water. Cooked in a tall closed pot, without gravy, jugged meat does not 'stew', but cooks moist and even. There would be just enough liquid when cooked to moisten the meat.

6 pigeons
1 head of celery, sliced
lemon slices, to garnish

For the stuffing:
**225 g (8 oz) fresh white
  breadcrumbs**

225 g (8 oz) suet, chopped
2.5 ml (1/2 tsp) salt
2.5 ml (1/2 tsp) pepper
2.5 ml (1/2 tsp) grated nutmeg
zest of 1 lemon
60 ml (4 tbls) chopped parsley
2 hard-boiled egg yolks, mashed
50 g (2 oz) butter, grated
1 egg, beaten

For the beurre manié:
25 g (1 oz) butter
25 g (1 oz) flour

Wash the pigeons and dry on absorbent paper. If you feel any lead shot in the skin, remove it. Mix the stuffing ingredients together, binding with the beaten egg. Divide into six and stuff each pigeon, sewing up the vents with needle and thread. Place in a very large jug with pieces of celery on top. Make the top of the jug airtight, using huff paste if necessary (see potted venison, p 18). Place the jug in a deep pan or metal pail, fill with boiling water to a point above the pigeons, and boil for 3 hours. To thicken the juices, make a beurre manié by kneading the butter and flour together with the fingers. Lay the birds on a heated dish. Pour the juices into a small pan and bring to the boil, adding little pieces of beurre manié until the gravy is thick. Pour the gravy over the birds, and garnish with slices of lemon.

Hannah Glasse:
The art of cookery made plain and easy

PRUNE SAUCE FOR LAND FOWL

450 g (1 lb) prunes
600 ml (21 fl oz) water
2.5 ml ('/2 tsp) ground ginger
2.5 ml ('/2 tsp) cinnamon
50 g (2 oz) sugar

Simmer the prunes in the water for about an hour until tender. Cool, then remove the stones. Boil the prunes and about 150 ml ('/4 pt) of the juice with the ginger, cinnamon and sugar for 2–3 minutes until thick, stirring constantly. Serve with chicken, turkey, duck or goose. Nott's recipe includes a little blood of the fowl.

John Nott:
The cook's and confectioner's dictionary

OYSTER LOAVES

Oysters were a favourite dish in the 18th century, and were often served as a garnish or sauce with meat. A common way of cooking them was to dip them in batter and deep-fry in lard. Oyster loaves make a pretty side dish for a first course.

4 underdone French rolls, each weighing about 50 g (2 oz)
100 g (4 oz) butter, melted
12 small fresh oysters
30 ml (2 tbls) white wine
a pinch of grated nutmeg
a pinch of ground mace

Preheat the oven to gas mark 7, 220°C, 425°F. Cut the tops off the rolls and scoop out most of the middles. Brush the undersides of the lids and the hollows of the loaves with melted butter. Toast in the oven until lightly golden. Sauté the oysters in the remaining hot butter for 2–3 minutes or until the edges curl. Add the wine and spices to the pan. Put 3 oysters and a little sauce in each hot roll, replace the lids and serve at once.

Hannah Glasse:
The art of cookery made plain and easy

'It was a bold man that first ate an oyster'

Jonathan Swift, *Polite conversation*, Dialogue 2

WHOLE FISH IN PASTRY

'Scale the Salmon, wash and dry him, chine him, and season him with Salt, Pepper, Ginger, Cloves, and Mace; lay him on a Sheet of Paste, and form it in the Shape of a Salmon, lay in Slices of Ginger, large Mace, and Butter upon the Fish, and turn up the other half of your Sheet of Paste on the Back, closing them on the Belly-side, from Head to Tail, bringing him into Proportion with Head, Fins, Gills, and Tail: Scale him, leave a Funnel to pour in Butter, and when it is bak'd, set it by to cool.'

1 whole fish, gutted and boned,
   but with head and tail left on,
   weighing about 450 g (1 lb)
salt and pepper
1.5 ml (¼ tsp) ground mace
2.5 ml (½ tsp) ground ginger or
   grated fresh ginger root

40 g (1½ oz) butter, cut into slivers
450 g (1 lb) shortcrust or puff
   pastry
1 raisin
1 egg white
15 ml (1 tbls) top of the milk

Wash the fish and dry with absorbent paper. Season it inside with the salt, pepper, mace and ginger, and insert slivers of butter. Roll out the pastry into a long oval, 5 cm (2 in) longer at each end than the fish, making sure it is wide enough to fold over the fish, with a spare 2.5–5 cm (1–2 in) to seal it. Transfer the fish carefully on to the pastry and place on the bottom half of the oval, its belly towards you. Fold the pastry over, and trim off the excess. Seal with water and crimp the edge. Adjust the shape of the tail and head if necessary. Transfer the fish to a foil-covered baking sheet.

To make scales: roll out the pastry trimmings, cut out oval scales, and, beginning at the tail end, stick them on with water in an overlapping design. Make a gill and fins, and stick in a raisin for an eye. Beat the egg white and milk together, then drizzle it over the pastry from a brush (brushing would flatten the scales too much). Bake in the top part of the oven at gas mark 6, 200°C, 400°F for 10 minutes until beginning to colour, then move it to the middle for 10 minutes, after which reduce the heat to gas mark 4, 180°C, 350°F to bake for a further 20 minutes. (If the fish is short and thick give it 10 minutes longer.) Serve hot or cold with pickled or sliced lemons. The dish may be decorated with sprigs of flowers or herbs.

John Nott:
The cook's and confectioner's dictionary

ANCHOVIES WITH PARMESAN CHEESE

'To make a nice whet before dinner, or a side dish for a second course. Fry some bits of bread about the length of an anchovy in good oil or butter, lay the half of an anchovy, with the bone upon each bit, and strew over them some Parmesan cheese grated fine, and colour them nicely in an oven, or with a salamander, squeeze the juice of an orange or lemon, and pile them in your dish and send to the table. This seems to be but a trifling thing but I never saw it come whole from the table.'

Brown your anchovies in the oven, or under the grill. 'The half of an anchovy' means half a fish, or two modern tinned 'fillets'.

William Verral: *The cook's paradise*

STEWED RED CABBAGE

This is an incredibly easy and tasty dish – you just have to be prepared for blue sausages!

I red cabbage, quartered and thinly sliced
450 g (I lb) sausages
4–6 slices smoked bacon, chopped
275 ml ('/2 pt) consommé or gravy
salt and pepper

Put cabbage, sausages, bacon, consommé (or gravy) and seasoning into a large saucepan. Bring to the boil then cook over a gentle heat for about 30–40 minutes, stirring occasionally, until sausages are cooked through and cabbage is tender.

Hannah Glasse:
The art of cookery made plain and easy

MELTED BUTTER SAUCE

This was the most usual sauce for vegetables.

10 ml (2 tsps) plain flour
150 ml ('/4 pt) water
a pinch of salt
50–75 g (2–3 oz) butter

In a small pan mix the flour, water and salt. Stir over gentle heat, without allowing it to boil. When hot, add the butter, cut into bits. Stir well until smooth. The sauce will not reheat, and if allowed to boil will taste raw. Sometimes a drop or two of lemon juice was added.

FRIED CELERY

Most vegetables were plain boiled and served with melted butter. The original of this recipe calls for several whole heads of celery, which were probably smaller than today.

125 g (5 oz) plain flour
2.5 ml ('/2 tsp) salt
1.5 ml ('/4 tsp) grated nutmeg
2 egg yolks
125 ml (4 fl oz) white wine
1 head of celery, weighing about
350 g (12 oz)
clarified butter (see p 37)

First make the batter: mix the flour, salt and nutmeg in a bowl, make a well in the centre and drop in the egg yolks with 15 ml (1 tbls) of the wine. Mix, stirring in the flour, then gradually add the remaining wine. Leave to stand. Cut the celery into 12.5 cm (5 in) lengths and simmer in boiling water until almost tender. Drain well and pat dry. Dip each piece in the batter to completely coat, then fry in hot clarified butter (or deep-fry in lard) for about 2 minutes on each side until golden.

Hannah Glasse:
The art of cookery made plain and easy

Mrs Glasse adds *'pour melted Butter over them'*!

POTATO PUDDING

Vegetables such as potatoes, carrots, spinach and artichokes were often used in place of a cereal thickener in sweet dishes, pies and puddings. This recipe makes a rich yet delicate pudding-pie, which is rather like a curd tart.

350 g (12 oz) puff pastry
450 g (1 lb) potatoes, cooked and mashed
100 g (4 oz) unsalted butter, softened
100 g (4 oz) caster sugar
2 eggs, beaten
2 egg yolks, beaten
60 ml (4 tbls) sherry or brandy
7 ml (1 rounded tsp) grated nutmeg
125 ml (4 fl oz) double cream
100 g (4 oz) currants

Roll out the pastry and use to line a 24 cm (9¹/₂ in) diameter, 5 cm (2 in) deep pie dish with a rim. Use the pastry trimmings to make a decorative border. Beat the remaining ingredients to a smooth batter and pour in. Place the dish above the middle of the oven and bake at gas mark 4, 180°C, 350°F for about 1 hour, or until risen and golden. Serve with hot wine sauce (see p 37). This is good hot or cold.

Hannah Glasse:
The art of cookery made plain and easy

Mrs Glasse advises that a stiffer mixture may be made with only 50 g (2 oz) butter, 3 egg yolks, 30 ml (2 tbls) liquor, formed into small cakes and fried in clarified butter.

SALAMANGUNDY

This magnificent salad was an opportunity for the cook to show her expertise in choosing a good balance of bland soft meats, sharp pickles, crisp vegetables and colourful leaves and flowers. Traditionally the ingredients were chopped small, and layered and heaped into a sugar-loaf shape, which mixed them all up together. This 1747 recipe reflects the new 'clean' taste in food: Mrs Glasse keeps each ingredient separate and recognisable in its own saucer, arranged on a large tray or platter, around a raised central dish. The spaces between the saucers are filled with watercress and flowers. The central raised dish is of chopped pickled herring. For the others you may choose a good balanced selection from the following:

cucumber, sliced very thin
apples, chopped small
onions, chopped small
celery, chopped small
crisp lettuce, finely shredded
peeled grapes
cooked French beans

pickled herring, chopped small
pickled gherkins, chopped small
pickled red cabbage
capers
lemons, sliced or chopped
anchovies

hard-boiled egg yolks
hard-boiled egg whites
cooked fowl, cut in strips or chopped

Hannah Glasse:
The art of cookery made plain and easy

BEETROOT PANCAKES

'A pretty corner dish for dinner or supper'

175 g (6 oz) peeled cooked beetroot
30 ml (2 tbls) brandy
45 ml (3 tbls) double cream
4 egg yolks
30 ml (2 tbls) plain flour
10 ml (2 tsps) caster sugar
5 ml (1 tsp) grated nutmeg
clarified butter (see p 37)

Mash the beetroot as finely as possible and mix with the other ingredients (or put all into a blender). Heat a shallow layer of clarified butter in a frying pan. Drop the beetroot mixture from the point of a tablespoon into the butter and shake the pan to flatten if necessary. Turn down the heat, as these burn very easily. Turn the pancakes over – they will cook quickly. Wipe out the pan if necessary between batches. These unusual delicate pancakes are good hot or cold. *'Garnish with green sweetmeats, preserved apricots or green sprigs of myrtle.'*

Elizabeth Raffald:
The experienced English housekeeper

A HEDGEHOG (not a real one!)

225 g (8 oz) ground almonds
15 ml (1 tbls) sweet sherry
5 ml (1 tsp) orange flower water
3 egg yolks
2 egg whites
150 ml (¼ pt) double cream
85 g (3 oz) granulated sugar
50 g (2 oz) butter
2 cloves or currants
100 g (4 oz) blanched almonds,
**   thinly sliced lengthwise**

Place all ingredients except the cloves or currants and sliced almonds in a large saucepan and mix together. Cook over a gentle heat, stirring constantly, until the mixture thickens sufficiently to hold its shape. Turn the mixture out onto a large plate and form into the shape of a hedgehog. Add eyes using cloves or currants, and spines using the chopped almonds. Surround the hedgehog with a sauce such as custard, or stewed fruit such as damsons, or apples cooked in red wine.

Hannah Glasse:
The art of cookery made plain and easy

STRAWBERRY FRITTERS

Plain fritters, made of ale, flour and eggs, were often eaten, but especially at Easter. These strawberry fritters are rather special.

**450 g (1 lb) large dry
   strawberries**
150 g (6 oz) plain flour
50 g (2 oz) caster sugar
10 ml (2 tsps) grated nutmeg
2 eggs, well beaten
225 ml (8 fl oz) single cream
lard for deep-frying
sugar, to finish

The strawberries must be dry. Leave the stalks on for easier handling. Sift the flour into a bowl and add the caster sugar and nutmeg. Make a well and drop in the eggs and cream. Then stir until all the flour and sugar are assimilated. Let the batter stand an hour or two. Dip each strawberry in batter until it is completely coated, and fry a few at a time in hot lard. Your lard must be hot enough to puff them, but not so hot as to brown them too quickly. Drain on absorbent paper and keep hot. Pile them in a pyramid in a hot dish and sprinkle sugar over. Decorate with leaves.

William Verral: *The cook's paradise*

Fresh pineapple and apple is also very good done this way. Any leftover batter may be dropped by the teaspoonful in lard to make delicious fritters.

CLARIFIED BUTTER

This is well worth doing. You will find it invaluable in modern cooking too. Once the buttermilk sediment has been removed from butter, it will keep indefinitely.

Melt 450 g (1 lb) of unsalted butter gently in a saucepan and let the first foam subside. Pour through a coffee filter paper, or simply let it stand, then pour off the clear butter into a keeping basin. When cold, remove any buttermilk from the bottom.

WINE SAUCE

This was the most usual sauce for puddings.

225 ml (8 fl oz) wine
50 g (2 oz) butter
30 g (1 1/4 oz) caster sugar

Mix the ingredients together and heat. Serve in a hot sauceboat. Lemon juice can be substituted for the wine.

To make a fine syllabub from the cow: 'Make your Syllabub of either Cyder or Wine, sweeten it pretty sweet, and grate Nutmeg in, then milk the Milk into the Liquor; when this is done, pour over the Top half a pint or Pint of Cream, according to the Quantity of Syllabub you make. You may make this Syllabub at Home, only have new Milk; make it as hot as Milk from the Cow, and out of a Tea-pot or any such Thing, pour it in, holding your Hand very high.'

Traditionally, syllabub was made by milking a cow into a bowl of ale or cider, which gave a frothy top to the liquor, and so it was partly eaten, partly drunk. Gradually in the 17th century, milk and ale were replaced by cream and wine, whipped together, which produced a creamy froth on a liquor base. During the 18th century, a new development was to increase the proportion of cream, so that no separation took place, and this 'everlasting syllabub' as it was called (really a modern whipped cream) existed side by side with the separated version throughout the 18th century. Thomas Turner of Hoathley near Lewes writes in his diary for Sunday 28 May 1758, *'Tho. Durrant, Tho. Davy and Mr Elless at our house in the even a-drinking of syllabub, Tho. Durrant finding milk, and we cider etc.'* And so it is clear that the original traditional milk syllabub was still enjoyed also. Special wooden cows were sold, from which to pour milk from a

height, in order to make a froth in the ale or cider. Whipped syllabub is the separated version made with cream.

90 ml (6 tbls) sherry, wine, cider, lemon or orange whey (see p 13), all sweet or sweetened juice and finely grated rind of 1 lemon
60 ml (4 tbls) sherry or white wine
50 g (2 oz) caster sugar
275 ml (1/2 pt) double cream

Put 15 ml (1 tbls) of the liquor or whey into each of six conical wine glasses. In a deep bowl, mix the lemon rind, juice, sherry or wine and sugar. Now, whisking all the time, with a hand whisk only, slowly add the cream. Keep whisking until soft peaks form. Do not overbeat. Just before serving, spoon into the glasses, laying the cream mixture carefully on top of the liquor.

Hannah Glasse:
The art of cookery made plain and easy

John Nott uses white wine for the liquor in his glasses plus the juice of raspberries, mulberries or black cherries.

To make everlasting syllabub, use the same whipped cream mixture as above, adding 5 ml (1 tsp) orange flower water. Put into glasses without any liquor in the bottom.

POTTED CHESHIRE CHEESE

This was a good way of improving a hard cheese and of preserving one that was about to go off. It actually improves with keeping.

225 g (8 oz) mature Cheshire cheese
50–75 g (2–3 oz) unsalted butter
30 ml (2 tbls) good sweet sherry
7 ml (1 rounded tsp) ground mace
clarified butter (see p 37)

Grate the cheese finely and mix with the butter, which should be soft but not melted. Add the sherry and mace, and mix well. Press well down in a pot, and cover with clarified butter.

Hannah Glasse:
The art of cookery made plain and easy

Port may be used in place of sherry. Eat sliced with walnuts and pears at the end of dinner.

RICH SEED CAKE

Caraway seeds were enormously popular in the later 18th century. This rich cake would be eaten at breakfast or afternoon tea among the gentry and middle classes. It was thought that the longer cakes were beaten the better – Mrs Raffald recommends beating this cake for 2 hours. Modern baking powder was not invented until the mid-19th century, so the success of a cake like this lies in its very careful technique. All ingredients and bowls must be slightly warmer than room temperature. Assemble all the ingredients before you begin, prepare the tin and preheat the oven.

225 g (8 oz) plain flour
5 ml (1 tsp) grated nutmeg
5 ml (1 tsp) grated cinnamon

25 g (1 oz) caraway seeds
225 g (8 oz) unsalted butter, softened
225 g (8 oz) caster sugar
4 eggs, separated, tepid

Line and grease a 20 cm (8 in) diameter, 7.5 cm (3 in) deep cake tin. Sift the flour and spices into a bowl, and add the caraway seeds. Make sure your mixing bowl is big enough, and slightly warm. Cream the butter and sugar in it very thoroughly, scraping the sides of the bowl. In a warm jug, beat the tepid egg yolks very well, then add the creamed mixture gradually, beating very well after each addition. With a scrupulously clean beater, beat the egg whites until they are stiff but not dry. Using a metal tablespoon, fold the beaten whites and the flour into the creamed mixture, about a fifth at a time; fold in by slicing the spoon edge gently down the middle, lifting and turning as lightly as possible, at the same time turning the bowl slowly with your other hand. The flour should be shaken in gently from a height. Stop as soon as the mixture appears amalgamated. Empty gently into the prepared tin and fork roughly level. Bake in the middle of the oven at gas mark 3, 170°C, 325°F for 1½ hours. Cool in the tin for 10 minutes, then turn on to a wire rack and remove the papers. The cake will be delicately crisp on the outside, and inside will have a light crumbly texture.

Elizabeth Raffald:
The experienced English housekeeper

PUNCH

A favourite 18th-century drink, brought from India in the late 17th century by merchants of the East India Company.

1.1 l (2 pt) claret
275 ml (½ pt) brandy
grated nutmeg, sugar and
**   lemon juice to taste**
toast, to serve

Mix the ingredients and serve in a punchbowl with toasted bread floating on the top. A variation of this was milk punch, where milk replaces the wine.

TEA CAUDLE

'Elegant enough for a supper table.'
Ale or wine caudles were traditional hot drinks, still taken at breakfast or supper until well into the 18th century. Tea caudle seems to be an innovation in the late 17th century when tea was first introduced from China. (Indian tea did not arrive until the 1830s.) Green China tea may be bought from specialist shops.

275 ml (¹/₂ pt) strong green China tea
15 ml (3 tsps) caster sugar
5 ml (1 tsp) grated nutmeg
1 egg yolk
125 ml (4 fl oz) white wine

Strain the tea into a small saucepan. Add the sugar and nutmeg and heat. In a small basin beat the egg yolk, add the wine and pour these into the hot tea, stirring continuously over gentle heat until very hot. Pour into a warmed caudle pot or china tea dishes.

Eliza Smith:
The compleat housewife, 1736 edition

Posset is a similar hot drink, but richer, being made with cream or milk.

Use the green tea leaves over again to make weak tea for drinking with slices of rich seed cake. Tea was so expensive that the leaves were often used twice.

History

CULINARY METHODS

Originally, cooking was done over a wood fire built on the floor of an open hearth. When coal was adopted as a fuel in the 16th century, however, the wrought-iron fire basket was developed, called in the 17th century the 'grate' or 'range'.

By 1700 the usual form of grate was a large oblong basket on four legs, fastened to the chimney back with tie bars, ideal for roasting large joints of meat. The spits rested on hooks on the two front legs and were usually turned mechanically by a clockwork spitjack, then later in the century by a smokejack sited inside the chimney and operated by the heat of the fire. The fire could be made smaller by winding adjustable sides or 'cheeks' inwards by a rack and pinion mechanism. Supports for pans, called trivets and fastened to the cheek tops, could swing out over the fire. Sometimes the top front bar let down, a 'fall bar', into a further ledge for pans. By the middle of the century in fashionable town houses, panels of cast iron were added to the front on each side, with flat iron plates on top to provide hobs.

Opposite: The dresser in the old kitchen at Audley End House, Essex

Roasting was the most important facility, as it was the most favoured method of cooking meat. Boiling came second, done in large pots hung over the fire. Stewing and sauce-making, where a gentle heat was required, had been done over little chafing dishes of charcoal on the floor of the hearth. From the late 17th century fashionable houses had a brick stove built into a corner of the kitchen, under a window for ventilation. Let into the top were small round fire baskets, about the size of chafing dishes, in which charcoal was burnt. This arrangement was much more convenient and comfortable for the cook than having to bend down to the hearth, though fumes were more of a problem than they had been in the draught of a chimney. As late as 1800, James Woodforde recorded in his diary on 22 July when his niece Nancy was making jam, 'she became giddy, too long at the stove where charcoal was burning, though the outward door was open all the time'.

Ovens were of masonry, and generally of a beehive shape built into the thickness of the wall. They had to be laboriously heated by building a fire inside the oven itself, then sweeping the hot ashes

Opposite: A kitchen range of the first half of the 18th century. Note the iron oven on the left, the clockwork spitjack, the two salamanders to the right, and the pudding cloth drying above

out and putting in the food to be baked. It was impossible to regulate the heat of the oven once the food was in. The development in mid-century of the iron oven with grate underneath, a 'perpetual oven', was of enormous benefit. One of the earliest recorded was the perpetual oven installed in Shibden Hall, Halifax, in 1750 for the Rev John Lister, for which he paid over four guineas.

Kitchen and scullery plans of the 1780s, Bretton Hall, West Yorkshire. The new boiler at the back of the range was to supply kitchen and scullery with hot water and steam for the warm closet and steam table, both of iron (extreme right: the pipe passes over the oven). It also supplied steam for the three kettles with taps (C) in the scullery. A is a double boiler with cast front and hob. B is a cast hot plate. The old oven and range were to be left intact. Note the new smokejack in the chimney

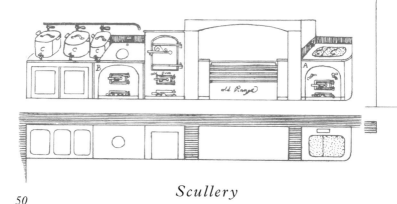

Scullery

Since the perpetual oven was often sited near the fireplace so that it could share the flue and chimney, it was a short step to combine oven and main fire. Accordingly, about 1770, in the north of England, one of the iron panels at the side of the grate was replaced by an iron oven, directly heated from the side of the fire. However, this tended to cook unevenly. A more expensive type was developed with flues running all round the oven and thence up the chimney. Then the iron panel at the other side of the grate was replaced by a water boiler, which was filled and emptied through the aperture in the hob top, and soon a tap was fitted to the front

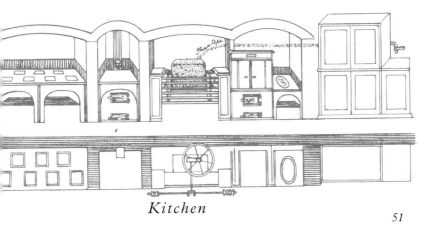

Kitchen

for even more convenience. On larger ranges, L-shaped boilers made use of the space at the side and behind the grate and very large boilers were put at the back, fed from a cistern with a ball-cock.

The fire was still open to the chimney, however, and a great deal of heat was lost. The criticism of Count Rumford who came from Bavaria in 1775 may have helped speed up the covering of the fire by a further iron plate, creating another useful simmering hob (and making the charcoal stove redundant), all the smoke being drawn through flues and up the chimney. The first patent for such a closed range was taken out in 1802.

Those without ovens sent their pies, stamped with the owner's initials, to the local bakery. Alternatively they could use screens or hasteners put close to the fire for meats, puddings, and some breads and cakes. In the metal Dutch oven with a polished tin interior to reflect the heat it was possible to roast the meat and bake a batter pudding at the same time. Thomas Turner, a Sussex shopkeeper, records that on Christmas day 1756 they had among other things 'a sirloin of beef roasted in the oven with a batter pudding under it'. Meanwhile the cauldron hanging on the reckon

Pat-a-cake, pat-a-cake, baker's man
Bake me a cake as fast as you can
Pat it and prick it and mark it with B
And put it in the oven for Baby and me

The majority of Georgian households cooked over open fires and didn't have ovens. They could roast meat, but were unable to bake bread or cakes. Instead, they took their bread or cake mix to the local baker to bake in his oven. To ensure they knew which loaf or cake was theirs they would mark it on the top with an initial.

Improved ovens allowed meat to be roasted and a batter pudding

baked at the same time, under the spit with the roasting meat to catch all the juices. This came to be known as a Yorkshire pudding, but it is not known whether the dish originated in Yorkshire.

A Dutch oven lined with polished tin

hook over the fire could efficiently boil joints of meat, puddings and nets of vegetables all in the same water.

Smaller houses of the period did not have a spit and irons for roasting meat. The poor man's spit was a danglespit suspended from the mantelpiece; this was nothing but a hook on a piece of string, from which the piece of meat spun before the fire. This was superseded by the clockwork bottlejack with a cast-iron balance wheel. On it were four hooks to spit four small birds or pieces of meat. The danglespit or bottlejack could also be mounted inside the Dutch oven, which had a door at the back for basting.

The majority of English people preferred plain food, roasted and boiled meat, puddings and pies, and so large varieties of kitchen utensils were not necessary. Those who wished to be fashionable, however, and could afford it, employed French cooks to make French dishes, and these required a more extensive *batterie de cuisine*. William Verral, who worked for M de Clouet, the chef of the Duke of Newcastle in Sussex, wrote a very readable and entertaining cookery book (*A Complete System of Cookery*, 1759). While purporting to be French in emphasis, in reality it sets out the solid English fare of the type he was producing for his customers at the White Hart in Lewes. He lists the utensils which every well-equipped kitchen of the well-to-do should have:

Stoves
2 boilers, one to hold a leg of Mutton, the other two fowls
A Soup-pot
Eight small Stew-pans, of different sizes, and their covers
Two very large [Stew-pans], and covers
A neat Frying-Pan
Two copper Ladles, tinned
3 large copper Spoons, tinned
2 Slices, tinned
An Egg-Spoon, tinned
A Pewter Cullendar
4 Sieves – one of Lawn
5 Copper-cups, to hold above ¹/4 of a Pint
6 Do. smaller
2 Etamines [for straining thick soup]
3 large wooden Spoons
Sauce-Pans, Several

Among other utensils he could have mentioned are: rolling pins, baking pins, cake hoops or tins, earthenware pans, bowls, knives, forks, graters, coffee mills, pestle and mortar, whisks, fritters, cabbage nets, pastry brush and jagging iron (marker), skimmer, salamander, fish kettle, lemon squeezer, writing paper, pudding cloths, weighing scales, spice and peppermills, patty pans, mustard bullet, jugs, dredgers, sugar cutters, baking spittle, toasting forks, dripping pans, larkspits and preserving pots.

Verral gives an amusing account of going to cook at a house in Sussex where the old gentleman typified many of his class in preferring his meat plain roast and boiled, and very little else. Although he was quite well-off, his kitchen had hardly anything but one frying pan and one sieve, and that had been used for sanding the floor.

The inventory of a Sussex farmer would bear out Verral's comment on the plainness of fare: the farmer had only 3 spits, 1 large iron skillet and a small brass one, an old iron kettle, 3 old iron porridge pots, 2 iron dripping pans, 1 old gridiron, 1 chopping knife, 1 old cleaver and 9 pewter dishes.

COOKERY BOOKS

From the late 17th century the increase of literacy, and the independence of mind which that gave, created a thirst for knowledge. Didactic books on every topic from health to geography, philosophy to gardening, were eagerly snapped up. Cookery books, which often included medical recipes and also directions for brewing and winemaking, were enormously popular. Between the years 1700 and 1800 over 300 titles on food and cookery alone were published, many of these going into several editions. It can be seen that, as countless thousands were produced, it was possible for every middle-class household to own at least one.

At the start of the century these books were mainly royal or court cookery, written by men who had served apprenticeships with French chefs who had worked at court or for the aristocracy. Many of the recipes in these books are French and elaborate, involving the use of expensive ingredients like truffles and morels, and the recipes are expressed in old-fashioned chef's jargon, difficult to understand.

Opposite: A gentleman's kitchen of 1727. Note the open hearth and the chicken being turned on the spit by the clockwork spitjack. After the engraving in Eliza Smith, *The Compleat Housewife*

The attitude to French cooking was ambivalent. It was considered very fashionable to hire a French chef (whose skill consisted largely in elaborate 'made dishes' using an extravagant special gravy called 'cullis'), and yet they, and French food, were scoffed at. 'So much is the blind Folly of this Age', writes Hannah Glasse, 'that [people] would rather be impos'd on by a French Booby, than give Encouragement to a good *English* Cook!' It must be remembered that Britain was at war with France for a large part of the 18th century, and patriotism and the idea of true-born Englishmen were important. It was thought that the plain roast beef of old England made plain stalwart Englishmen.

Perhaps the preference for plainness is one reason why it is the cookery books written by women which succeeded so spectacularly, notably those by Eliza Smith (1st edition 1727), Hannah Glasse (1st edition 1747) and Elizabeth Raffald (1st edition 1769).

Mrs Glasse's *The Art of Cookery made Plain and Easy* went into no fewer than 17 editions between 1747 and 1803, and all other cook-books pirated her recipes (as she herself had pirated from

Opposite: The cook whisks syllabub, watched by a servant girl through the window of the cook's room next door

> ## 'Oh! The roast beef of England. And old England's roast beef'
>
> Henry Fielding, *Grub Street Opera III*, 3

Eliza Smith and others). Mrs Glasse's recipes are more detailed in measures and method than those of her predecessors. She wrote out her recipes very clearly and precisely, so that even an untutored cook-maid could understand them: 'I have attempted a Branch of Cookery which Nobody has yet thought worth their while to write upon ... My Intention is to instruct the lower Sort [so that] every servant who can read will be capable of making a tolerable good Cook.'

Mrs Glasse's book reflects the preferred simplicity in cooking and also the new standards of hygiene, due in part to piped water in some parts of towns. The cleanliness of London servants was remarked on by foreign visitors. She gives instructions on how to clean spits, gridirons, wooden bowls and other cooking utensils with sand and hot water only (soap would leave a flavour).

MEALS

The new recipe books were for the gentry, the professional middle classes and richer tradesman class, and were an encouragement to aspire to a higher standard of living.

The times of dinner gradually began to change. In the early 18th century the middle classes and the higher orders might breakfast at 9am or 10am and have nothing else before dinner, which was usually at 2 or 3pm. As the century progressed, dinner time got later, so that by the late 18th century dinner was generally at 6 or 7pm. This left a long gap which was filled by the

Teatime in the middle of the afternoon was a Georgian innovation because of the move away from dinner at 2pm or 3pm, which was usual at the beginning of the 18th century, to a large meal taken at 6pm or 7pm. To stave off hunger in between breakfast and dinner, therefore, fashionable society began to take 'afternoon tea' with cakes and biscuits at 4pm.

new development of afternoon tea. The less fashionable classes who continued to have dinner in the middle of the day had a dish of tea in the afternoon, then had supper in the evening of cold meats, cold pies, bread and cheese.

Many cookery books have diagrams of dinner table layouts, which vary from the modest to the lavish (royal or aristocratic layouts on a massive scale appear in only a few early books, all by men). The dishes for each course were to be placed very correctly and symmetrically on the table.

The first course to be arranged on the table always consisted mainly of meats, roasted, boiled, stewed and fried, some with sauces. Vegetables do not generally appear except as a garnish to the meat. Bread was handed round. Soup, if it was on the bill of fare, was served and eaten first, then removed and a fish dish put in its place. After fish, the meat, which must by then have cooled considerably, was served. One writer, John Trusler, advises removing the cold fat that swims upon the gravy in cold weather.

The first course was then removed and the second put in its place. This consisted of lighter dishes of meat and fish, with the

Opposite: Making salamangundy

addition of sweet pies, puddings and tarts. Little side dishes of biscuits and pickles stayed on the table throughout the meal. After the second course, the cloth was removed and dessert followed – jellies, sweetmeats, fruit, nuts and cheese (though jellies and sweetmeats were sometimes placed in the centre of the second course). After the dessert had been removed, and a glass or two of wine drunk, the ladies withdrew, leaving the men to their drinking. Then the men would join the ladies for conversation or card games.

Rules for behaviour during the meals were set out by John Trusler in *The Honours of the Table*, 1788, which gives us a glimpse of the etiquette then current among the upper middle classes, gentry and aristocracy. Guests were to walk into the dining room in strict order of rank, ladies first. The mistress sat at the top end of the table among all the women, with the most important female guests next to her. The master sat among the men in order of rank at the bottom end of the table. At the time Trusler was writing, however, a new mode of seating was gaining in preference, whereby the ladies and gentlemen sat alternately, though still in order of rank. As the old segregated arrangement went out, so did the boisterous drinking of healths and bumpers and loyal toasts. Male joviality became tempered with female sensibility.

At the beginning of the century the English hostess did all the carving and serving, thereby missing food and conversation herself. By mid-century a new 'French ease' became fashionable

The Gourmets, plate 9 from 'Comforts of Bath', 1798, by Thomas Rowlandson

whereby the master and mistress carved the dishes that were before them at each end of the table, and helped guests to these. Then the guests helped themselves and each other to the rest. By the turn of the 19th century when Mrs Rundell was writing, even this fashion had declined, guests had ceased to help themselves, and food was now served by the servants.

Trusler instructs the guests to behave properly. It is vulgar to eat too quickly or too slowly, which shows you are either too hungry or you don't like the food. It is also vulgar to eat your soup with your nose in the plate. You must avoid 'smelling to the meat whilst on the fork' – it shows you suspect the meat is tainted. 'It is

> 'Coleridge declares that a man cannot have a good conscience who refuse apple dumplings, and I confess that I am of the same opinion'
>
> Charles Lamb 1775

exceedingly rude to scratch any part of your body, to spit, or blow your nose … to lean your elbows on the plate, to sit too far from it, to pick your teeth before the dishes are removed.' If the necessity of nature obliged you to leave the table, you had to steal away unobserved, and return without announcing where you'd been. Chamberpots had been kept in or just outside the dining room, but the new delicacy of feelings shrank from such crudeness.

Jonathan Swift wrote a satirical handbook (*Directions to Servants*, 1745) in which he 'recommends' bad, slovenly practices. From these we may infer that servants had subtle ways of getting even with their masters and mistresses. For instance he tells the cook, if her mistress does not allow her the usual perquisite of the dripping, to use it now and then along with expensive butter to enliven the fire; to take half the meat and share it with the butler in exchange for the butler's wine; if a lump of soot falls in the soup, to stir it well in to give the soup a high *French* taste; if dinner is late, to put the clock back; to comb her hair over the cooking, so that she can keep her eye on it while grooming herself – if the master complains about hair in the food, to say it's the footman's; if a chicken leg disappears (into the butler) to say a dog got it.

INGREDIENTS

How did 18th-century food differ from that of the preceding century? Because of the increasing use of sugar, which made food more palatable, many of the old spices, flavourings and colourings, such as ambergris and musk, saffron and sanders (red), went out of fashion, as also did native potherbs like daisies and violets. Raw green sauces and mashed herbs and vinegar were replaced by pickles, ketchups and, later in the century, bottled sauces. Other concoctions were disappearing: spiced wines like hippocras, and the wilder gothic mixtures of Stuart cookery, where there might be 20 or 30 ingredients elaborately mixed up, such as battalia pie with its crenellated turrets filled with exotica.

Food became simpler; for example there were new sauces tasting of one thing only: parsley or mustard or anchovy. But the universal sauce for vegetables was melted butter sauce (see p 29) usually served in over-generous amounts. Thomas Turner, dining at his uncle's on 17 October 1756, had roasted pig and very good turnips, 'but spoiled by almost swimming in butter and also a butter pond pudding and that justly called, for there was almost but enough in it to have drowned the pig, had it been alive'. Butter, in spite of its expense, was used lavishly in almost every dish.

One of the biggest changes was brought about by advances in agriculture. At the beginning of the century, cattle had to be killed at the start of winter because there was no fodder, and so salt meat was eaten until the following spring or summer. Now winter feeding practices were copied from Dutch farmers, and cattle could be kept through the winter. Enclosure of land and improved breeding with superior strains from Holland meant that the quality of meat improved dramatically, though this did not happen

on a wide scale until the end of the century. Farm animals began to replace wild in the nation's diet, especially as game became more and

A dogspit in use

more the prerogative of the landowner, through enclosures and severe game laws.

Foreign visitors were amazed at English meat-eating. What M Misson said in the 1690s held true (except for the poorer people) for the whole of the 18th century:

> I always heard that they [the English] were great flesh-eaters, and I found it true. I have known people in England that never eat any bread, and universally they eat very little; they nibble a few crumbs, while they chew meat by whole mouthfuls … Among the middling sort of people they had 10 or 12 sorts of common meats which infallibly takes their turns at their tables, and two dishes are their dinners: a pudding, for instance, and a piece of roast beef.

Habits in fish-eating changed. Improved transport by the end of the century meant that sea fish could be carried to the towns in barrels of sea water comparatively quickly, and so many freshwater fish, with their muddier taste, went out of favour, with only the better species such as carp, pike and eel remaining popular. Fish ponds gradually became redundant and were turned into ornamental ponds. Oysters were plentiful and were eaten in large numbers.

Pudding was an English phenomenon. It took the place of cereal pottage as a starchy filler, and by the 1740s roast beef and plum pudding had become a national dish. At one time puddings were boiled only in the clean guts of newly slaughtered animals, but the increased use of the pudding cloth meant that pudding could be made at any time and the varieties proliferated so that foreign visitors were astonished. M Misson wrote:

> They bake them in the oven, they boil them with the meat, they make them 50 several ways: BLESSED BE HE THAT INVENTED PUDDING, for it is a manna that hits the palates of all sorts of people ... [and they] are never weary of it.

The wonderfully versatile suet pudding could be filled with beefsteak, giblets, pigeon, duck, raw fruit, currants and great ponds of butter. Boiled and baked puddings could be of rice, oatmeal, vermicelli, sago or custard. Sweet baked puddings, often cooked in puff pastry crust, were somewhat more elegant, and could be made with such things as curds, fruit, potatoes, carrots, spinach, custard, bread and butter, dried fruit and almonds.

Thomas Turner has as many as three puddings at once. On 15 November 1759 his dinner is 'a fine piece of beef roasted, a currant pond pudding, a currant suet pudding and a butter pudding cake' (all boiled).

The other filler, bread, as noted by Misson, was eaten sparingly by the well-off, but it was eaten increasingly by the poor. In the Midlands and south white bread became available for the first time to the poor, who then scorned rougher bread when bad harvests struck later in the 18th century. Cake was eaten at breakfast and afternoon tea. The traditional raising agent was wet ale yeast, then eggs were added, but eggs alone were soon found to be effective in raising a cake.

The most common vegetables were cabbage, turnips and carrots, along with parsnips and onions. Potatoes were not eaten every day, except in Ireland and parts of the north-west. Green vegetables, which had once been eaten in cereal pottages, were now simply boiled with melted butter sauce. Garden peas, French beans, asparagus, artichokes, cauliflower and celery were enjoyed by the well-off as were green salad things in summer: lettuce, cress, cucumber, spring onions. Tomatoes began to appear in recipes in the late 18th century, but were not eaten raw until the end of the 19th.

Improved seed from Holland meant better varieties of vegetables and fruit. Hothouses permitted the growing of grapes and peaches and even pineapples for the privileged. Raw fruit was at last acknowledged by medical opinion to be safe; at one time thought to cause colic and spread plague, now it was eaten as a healthy food. Garden rhubarb, introduced from Italy in the 17th century, was put into English tarts in the late 18th. Raw fruit was made into wine, with the help of cheaper sugar. Fruit was bottled and made into jam, which was cheaper than butter as a spread for bread. Favourite fruits were damsons and gooseberries, and the favourite garnish was lemons.

Coffee, chocolate and tea had been introduced in the late 17th century.

> 'A cucumber should be well sliced, and dressed with pepper and vinegar, and then thrown out, as good for nothing'

Samuel Johnson, *Tour of the Hebrides*

Chocolate was at first mixed with wine, then water. It came in a cake or roll, and had to be grated into hot liquid, then swizzled with a notched stick called a chocolate mill (it was not made into chocolate bars until the end of the century). All three beverages were drunk sweetened, as people were used to sugaring their wine. Coffee was drunk mainly by the well-to-do; it was expensive and could not be faked. Tea, from China, was so expensive that it was kept in a locked caddy. Consequently, it was drunk very weak, sweetened and at first without milk. However, both tea and coffee were recognised as stimulant drugs, and it was thought the addition of milk would lessen the deleterious effects. Because of the high customs duties on tea, smuggling was carried out on a large scale. Parson Woodforde records in his diary, 29 March 1777:

> Andrews the Smuggler brought me this night about 11 o'clock a bag of Hyson tea 6 pound weight. He frightened us a little by whistling under the parlour window just as we were going to bed. I gave him some Geneva and paid him for the tea 10s 6d per pound.

Coffee, chocolate and tea necessitated new special cups and pots, kettles and urns, which stimulated the pottery and metalware industries. Making and taking tea became an elegant ceremony at which the mistress of the house could show off her pretty china. In 1717 Thomas Twining opened the first Tea Shop for Ladies (in imitation of coffee shops for men) and in the 1720s the first tea garden was opened in the old Vauxhall Gardens in London and this soon became very fashionable.

Charles II had grown accustomed to tea drinking during his exile, and he and his queen, Catherine of Braganza, popularised the drink among the wealthier classes after the Restoration. Tea was initially so expensive that it was kept in a locked caddy and dispensed by the mistress of the house. But its use and popularity speedily spread, and the

average of 40,000 pounds imported in 1699 quickly grew to around 240,000 pounds in 1708. By the end of the 18th century it was a very popular drink at all levels of society.

Above: A silver tea-kettle with spirit lamp
Left: Detail from *Tea time,* 1779, engraving by Taylor after Wale

Because of improved transport, regional specialities such as Scotch salmon, Newcastle salted haddock and Cheddar, Gloucester, Cheshire and Stilton cheeses came to be widely known. Foreign food included sea turtles from the West Indies (those who could not afford it made mock turtle dishes), sago from Malaya, vermicelli, macaroni and Parmesan from Italy, piccalilli, punch, curry, rice, pilau and pickled mangoes from India, and ketchups from the Far East (China and Malaya). Ketchups were imitated, and bottled sauces were produced commercially at the end of the century, the first being Lazenby's anchovy essence and Harvey's sauce. Ready-mixed curry powder was on sale from the 1780s.

Butcher's meat was cheap, but butter was double the price of meat (which would make it £3 a pound today). The prices recorded by the Rev J Ismay in 1755 in Mirfield, West Yorkshire, are typical: beef, mutton and veal were 2½d to 3d a pound, butter 5d to 6d and cheese 3d to 4d, while a roasting pig was 2s, a Christmas goose or turkey 2s 6d, a hen 7d and ducks 8d. In 1756 Thomas Turner in Sussex was paying ½d more for these things, saying they were dear. Cheshire cheese was as much as 5½d a pound. In 1759

Turner paid 9s 3d for a pound of green tea, and in 1777 Parson Woodforde paid 10s 6d, though tea could fetch as much as 3 guineas a pound. A bottle of ordinary wine was 2s. Truffles for the privileged cost in the 1730s £1 to £1 10s a pound. But it was the price of wheat which fluctuated most and had the most effect on the poor.

Comparing the prices with wages shows that working men could not afford to eat well: weavers earned only 5d a day, tailors only 6d plus food, farm labourers 7d, day labourers 1s, carpenters and masons 1s 3d. Shopkeepers, tradesmen and master craftsmen might get £1 a week and could afford to eat meat every day. Wages in London were higher but then so were prices.

In 1786 John Trusler in *The London Adviser and Guide* reports that fowl and game were extremely expensive: ducks were 3s each, chickens 3s 10d, geese 5s and a brace of partridge 3s 6d. Mackerel, which you could buy in Billingsgate for 4d or 5d a pound, was 1s 3d in town and even 2s 6d when sold to houses in fashionable squares.

Some members of the aristocracy still found it important to display their wealth and power on a massive scale, one instance being the Earl of Warwick's outdoor banquet for 6,000 in 1746, described by Horace Walpole. The court was not so ostentatious. In view of the patriotism attached to the roast beef of old England it is not surprising to discover that the king and his court at St James's Palace, when not entertaining, ate rather plain food. Stephen Mennell has discovered that the daily royal menus, as set down in the papers of Lord Stewart of the Royal Household, were not so different from the company menus of the country gentlemen, consisting mainly of roast and boiled meat. In 1740, when Paris was getting '*nouvelle cuisine*', George II and his household were eating good plain English fare (though a few French names for dishes were thrown in for effect).

A gentleman now had for breakfast – instead of ale and cereal pottage – tea, coffee, chocolate (the last going out of fashion as the century advanced), whigs (rich bread rolls), buttered toast or cake. Sometimes he had broth or water gruel.

Supper was taken by those who had dined at midday. It usually consisted, at least among the tradesman class, of cold meats, cold pies and tarts. A typical company supper in February 1758, enjoyed with his neighbours by Turner, consisted of cold roast beef, cold roast goose, cold neat's tongue, cold apple pasty, bread and cheese. After these suppers, Turner and his wife usually played at cards, winning or losing as much as five shillings, and drank into the early hours of the morning. He was frequently drunk, and his over-indulgence typifies the widespread drunkenness which affected all classes in the 18th century.

Strong drink was cheap and widely available. Because of the troubles with France which started in the late 17th century, French wines and brandy became scarce and expensive (and widely smuggled), and Portuguese and Spanish wines were drunk instead. However, the government, in the hopes of reducing smuggling, encouraged the production of home-made wines and brandy. This was so successful, and spirits were so cheap, that scenes such as that depicted by Hogarth in *Gin Lane* were common, with the gin shop notice declaring 'drunk for a penny, dead drunk for two-pence, clean straw for nothing'. In Scotland even the poor drank neat whisky with their meals.

Gambling too was common. It was at the gaming table that the sandwich was invented, when in 1760 John Montague, 4th Earl of Sandwich, called for his meat to be put between two pieces of bread so that he could carry on playing uninterrupted.

Gin drinking during the 18th century, particularly among the poorer classes, became a craze. Known as Geneva from the French word for juniper, genièvre, it was cheap and widely available. In 1730 over six and a half million gallons of 'official' gin a year were consumed, on top of the quantities of illegal, often dangerously adulterated, gin bought from illicit suppliers, and by 1750 the annual total was over eleven million gallons. In 1751 over 9,000 children died after being given gin to keep them quiet.

In all classes drunkenness and gambling went together, along with rough or cruel sports, typifying a callousness which was reflected in the cruel treatment of creatures intended for food. Living fish were slashed to make the flesh contract. This was called 'crimping'. Eels were skinned alive, lobsters roasted alive, crammed poultry were sewn up in the guts, turkeys were suspended by the feet and bled to death from the mouth, bulls were baited before slaughter to make the meat more tender, pigs and calves were lashed for the same reason. One of William Kitchiner's recipes begins, 'Take a red cock that is not too old and beat him to death.' Towards the end of the century growing sensibility about humanitarian principles caused increasing revulsion against these cruelties.

A century of unbridled appetite took its toll on health. Such massive amounts of protein, animal fat and alcohol, in the absence of fibrous vegetables or coarse bread, coupled with a sedentary existence (and smoking) caused problems. The high proportion of salt meat eaten in Scotland helped cause heart disease there. Degenerative diseases such as gout, diabetes, apoplexy (heart attack) and cirrhosis of the liver were common. Health hydros and spas became fashionable. At Bath, many people took the waters during the day, only to debauch themselves in the gay social whirl of dinners, balls and theatres at night.

Parson Woodforde was one of those who indulged themselves. His diet was a heavy one with too much meat, too few vegetables and too many puddings, cakes and pies, so that he suffered from the common complaints of heartburn, colic, bleeding piles and gout. When his gout got unbearable, he took water gruel for supper.

The labouring classes in the Midlands and south fared badly. They lived on bought bread and cheese, enlivened with a few potatoes and washed down with tea, which by the end of the century had become a necessity to them, to replace the now expensive beer that had once supplied them with both calories and vitamins. Deficiency diseases such as scurvy and rickets increased towards the end of the century, especially in towns.

'The vulgar boil, the learned roast, an egg'

Alexander Pope,
Imitations of Horace, 1738

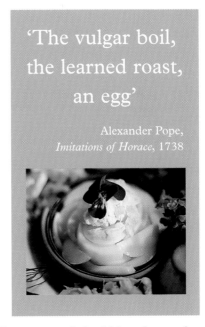

In Wales and the north the diet was much healthier, the staples being barley or oats. Nutritionists have now discovered the enormous benefits of fibrous foods and of oats in particular in protecting against degenerative diseases.

There were also many hazards in 18th-century kitchens. Apart from the ever-present danger from fire, scalding and fumes, there were perils in the utensils themselves. Brass and copper pans, if used with acid food, could create poisonous verdigris. 'A whole family died', writes Hannah Glasse, 'owing to verdi-grease.' Even so, some fruits and pickles were deliberately cooked in these vessels in

Substitutes for Bread, or Right Honourables Saving the Loaves & Dividing the Fishes, 1795, by James Gillray: Georgian political caricature showing the Prime Minister William Pitt and his cabinet feasting during a food shortage crisis

J.ᵗ Gᵗ diet f.ᵗ **SUBSTITUTES**
To the Charitable Committee, for reducing the
Hard shifts made by the Framers & Signers

order to achieve a bright green colour. Alum and boiling vinegar were used to make apples green, although too much could upset the stomach. Peach-laurel leaves were used to impart a bitter almond flavour, which was safe only if the food was brought to a boil. Used tea-leaves were sold by servants to dealers who recoloured them, often with poisonous materials, and then sold them on. Bad meat, stale fish, rancid butter and spoiled fruit and vegetables were traps that lay in wait for the unwary shopper, and many cookery books had an important section on how to choose the best market stuff. They also had recipes on how to rescue bad meat with vinegar and spices – a rather dangerous practice – for example Hannah Glasse's recipe on how 'to save potted birds, that begin to be bad'.

Fresh food was kept in cellars or larders, but it could not be kept long – less than a week. A great deal of preserving took place. Jam and pickles, fruit and vegetables were put up in glass or earthenware jars sealed with paper or leather, though there was always the possibility of botulism since the jars were not then boiled. Meat, fish and shellfish were potted or baked in a crust and kept for several weeks airtight under a sealing layer of clarified fat. Hams and bacon were cured, beef and mutton were salted. Meats, fish, sausages and puddings were smoked, hung in the chimney over a wood or peat fire (coal smoke was not suitable). The Scots had fresh meat for only five months of the year, August to December, living off salt beef and mutton the rest of the time.

The idea of ice as a preserving agent had been introduced from the Continent in the late 17th century. Fashionable people built ice-houses in their grounds, where ice lasted most of the year. Ice-creams were a speciality for those with ice-houses.

> 'I think I could eat one of Bellamy's veal pies'
>
> William Pitt the Younger, British statesman, last words, attrib

Modern readers of 18th-century recipes may well be mystified by some of the weights and measures. It soon becomes clear when making recipes that a 'spoonful' is roughly equivalent to a modern standard tablespoon, and that 'a teaspoon' is bigger than a modern teaspoon, that is it was one used for measuring tea, not for stirring. 'A glass' is roughly 4 fluid ounces and 'a pint' is a wine pint, that is

16 fluid ounces rather than 20 fluid ounces as today (the pint changed to imperial in the 19th century; America has kept the old measure). The pound in most districts was the same as today, but a stone, when referring to meat, was 8 lb. A peck of flour was 2 gallons, or 14 lb, and a peck loaf was 17 lb 6 oz(!), the half peck loaf 8 lb 11 oz, and the most usual size, the quartern loaf, was 4 lb 5 oz (by comparison, the modern 'large loaf' is 1³/₄ lb). A penny white loaf, according to Elizabeth David, was 6 oz in the early 18th century, though this varied with the price of wheat – it could be as little as 3–4 oz. The penny brown loaf was about three times heavier. It is evident from shorter cooking times that fowl were generally smaller, and eggs were equivalent to our smallest modern eggs (size 4). (For those wishing to translate the above weights into metric, one pound is 450g and one ounce is 25g.)

Some of these recipes will taste unfamiliar, but are no less enjoyable for that. The overwhelming impression on the taste buds is one of butter, wine and the ubiquitous nutmeg, which seems to have been the Georgians' national flavouring.

BIBLIOGRAPHY

Anon, *Adam's luxury, and Eve's cookery*, 1744, reprinted by Prospect Books (London, 1983)

Bradley, Richard, *The country housewife and lady's director*, 6th edn, London, 1736, reprinted with an introduction by Caroline Davidson and glossary by Prospect Books (London, 1980)

Carter, Charles, *The complete practical cook*, 1730, reprinted by Prospect Books (London, 1984)

Cook, Ann, *Professed cookery*, 2nd edn, Newcastle 1775; 3rd edn reprinted as *Ann Cook and Friend*, with introduction and notes by Regula Burnet, by Oxford University Press (London, 1936)

Glasse, Hannah, *The art of cookery made plain and easy*, 1747, reprinted with glossary and index by Prospect Books (London, 1983)

Maclean, Virginia, *A short-title catalogue of household and cookery books published in the English tongue 1701–1800*, Prospect Books (London, 1980)

Mennell, Stephen, 'Food at the late Stuart and Hanoverian courts', *Petits Propos Culinaires*, Vol 17, pp 22–9

Nott, John, *The cook's and confectioner's dictionary*, 3rd edn, London, 1726, reprinted by Lawrence Rivington (London, 1980)

Raffald, Elizabeth, *The experienced English housekeeper*, 10th edn, Manchester, 1786; 8th edn, 1782, reprinted by E and W Books (Publishers) Ltd (1970) and Redwood Press for Paul Minet reprints (1972)

Smith, Eliza, *The compleat housewife*, London, 1727; 15th edn, 1753, reprinted with a foreword by Lord Montagu of Beaulieu, and the addition of a glossary compiled by C H Hudson, by Literary Services and Production Ltd (London, 1968)

Stead, Jennifer, 'Quizzing Glasse: or Hannah scrutiniz'd', *Petits Propos Culinaires*, Vol 13, pp 9–24, Vol 14 pp 17–30

Swift, Jonathan, *Directions to servants in general* (London, 1745)

Trusler, John, *The honours of the table, or, rules for behaviour during meals* (London, 1788)

Verral, William, *The cook's paradise*, London, 1759, reprinted with Thomas Gray's cookery notes in holograph, with an introduction and appendices by R L Megroz, by Sylvan Press (London, 1948)

Wilson, C Anne, *Food and drink in Britain*, Constable London, 1973; Penguin Books (Harmondsworth, 1984)

ACKNOWLEDGEMENTS

The publishers would like to thank Lace Wars 18th-century Re-enactment Group for their help in preparing this book, in particular Alison Smith and Caro Heyworth for cooking and presenting a number of the recipes. We would also like to thank James O. Davies and Peter Williams for their superb photography.

The publishers would like to thank the following people and organisations listed below for permission to reproduce the photographs in this book. Every care has been taken to trace copyright holders, but any omissions will, if notified, be corrected in any future edition.

All photographs are © English Heritage.NMR with the exception of the following:
Front cover: Whitworth Art Gallery, The University of Manchester, UK/Bridgeman Art Library; p 19 Private Collection/Bridgeman Art Library; p 67 Victoria Art Gallery, Bath and North East Somerset Council/Bridgeman Art Library; p 79 Derry Brabbs; p 88 Courtesy of the Warden and Scholars of New College, Oxford/Bridgeman Art Library

Line illustrations by Peter Brears

RECIPE INDEX

Other titles in this series:

Roman Cookery

Medieval Cookery

Tudor Cookery

Stuart Cookery

Victorian Cookery

Ration Book Cookery

" Fresh Oysters! penny a lot!"

Sirloin of Beef Roſt

Veal
Escalopps
&
Lemons

Fry'd
Sallary

Green
Peas
Soop
—Remove—
Fish
baked in
Pastry

Stew'd
Venison

Oyster
Loaves

Turkey bo'd
&
Prune Sauce